This edition published by Barnes & Noble, Inc,
by arrangement with Michelle Lovric
2000 Barnes & Noble Books
ISBN 0-7607-2199-8

Weird Wills & Eccentric Last Wishes
Designed by Lisa Pentreath and Michelle Lovric
copyright © 2000 Michelle Lovric
Editorial Assistant: Kristina Blagojevitch
Printed in China by Imago

9 8 7 6 5 4 3 2

ACKNOWLEDGEMENTS
The editor gratefully acknowledges
the assistance of the following
people: Iain Campbell and Judith
Grant. With particular thanks
to Joanna Skepers for her help
and inspiration in all things,
particularly these.

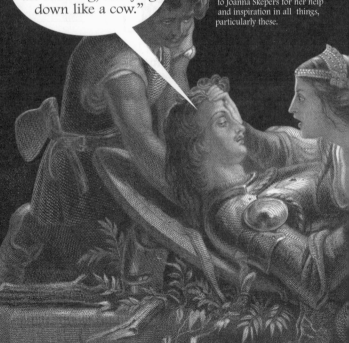

Siward, the warrior
Earl of Northumberland
(?—1055) said:

"Lift me up that I may
die standing, not lying
down like a cow."

Weird Wills

& Eccentric Last Wishes

edited by Michelle Lovric

BARNES
& NOBLE
BOOKS
NEW YORK

Death can make even triviality momentous and delirium oracular.

Edward Le Comte

Editor's Note

A will is the last statement we make, our last definition of ourselves and our desires. The way we dispose our earthly disposition says an enormous amount about us. No one makes a will without the knowledge that it will be read after his death, when it is too late to change it. The will lives on after him: no insult can be withdrawn, no eccentricity diminished, no gift re-allocated. Over the centuries, wills have been used to deliver surprises, slaps in the face, generosity and blessings from beyond the grave. On these pages is a small selection of some of the most amusing and interesting wills published during the past two millennia.

Last words are often less considered, as they are frequently delivered in the extremes of suffering. Their piquancy depends on the circumstances of the final scenes. Great bravery has been shown; shameful cowardice and ridiculous misconception, too. It should be noted that many different last words have been attributed to famous people. As the witnesses are generally few, and distressed, it is difficult to establish the truth in these cases. Horatio Nelson is a good example.

The last words of the great English naval commander, as he lay dying during the Battle of Trafalgar, have been variously reported as: *"Kiss me, Hardy. Thank God, I have done my duty!"* and *"Don't throw me overboard!"*

A deathbed's a detector of the heart.

Edward Young

Contents

Botched Conclusions

The British politician Henry John Temple, the third Viscount Palmerston (1784—1865) was either mistakenly optimistic, or irrepressibly witty till the last. His final words were:

"Die, my dear doctor! that's the last thing I shall do."

"I can't sleep."

James M. Barrie (1860—1937), author of Peter Pan, was wrong. These were his last words.

"I think I could eat one of Vulliamy's pork pies."

said the 18th-century politician William Pitt. Other sources claim that his last words were rather more dignified:

"Always my country. How I love my country."

King William II (1087—1100) was out hunting
with his friend, Walter Tirel. He urged Tirel:

"Shoot! Walter, in heaven's name!"

Tirel did shoot and his arrow killed the king.

8

"Are you sure it's safe?"

William Palmer (1824—56), the infamous
poisoner, when mounting the gallows.

Goodbye, Cruel World

"I am disgusted with everything."

A suicide note left by the French surrealist poet René Crevel
(1901—35).

The last words uttered by the Italian writer Gabriele D'Annunzio
(1863—1938) were to his chauffeur:

"I'm bored ... I'm bored."

"I see no reason why
the existence of
Harriet Martineau
should be perpetuated."

Harriet Martineau (1802—76), English writer.

"Do not leave me
in suspense!"

Convicted of treason and sentenced to
death, Henri de Talleyrand de Chalais
(1599—1626) thus urged the
executioner to expedite his task.

"I shall hear in Heaven."

Ludwig van Beethoven (1770—1827).
The brilliant German composer tragically became
deaf in later life. He died during a violent hailstorm,
shaking his fist at the heavens.

"Nothing but death."

This was the response given by the English novelist Jane Austen
(1775—1817), when asked, in her final months of illness,
if there was anything she wanted.

Washington Irving (1783—1859),
American man of letters, said:

"Well, I must arrange my pillows for another night. When will this end?"

Cotton Mather (1663—1728),
English-American divine and writer, said:

"Is this dying? Is this all? Is this all
I feared when I prayed
against a hard death?
Oh, hear this! I can bear it!
I am going to where
all tears will be wiped
from my eyes."

Dr William Hunter (1718—83), Scottish physiologist
and physician, spoke these reassuring words:

"If I had strength to hold a pen,
I would write down how easy
and pleasant a thing it is to die."

"I have such sweet thoughts."

Prince Albert (1819—61), Consort of Queen Victoria.

Looking at a sunset, the Irish-born
American sculptor Augustus
Saint-Gaudens (1848—1907) observed:

"It's very beautiful,
but I want to go
farther away."

Last Regrets

Dr Forbes Winslow, an Anglo-American doctor, reported on the unusual case of a jilted lover, who had lived a miserable and lonely life. In his will, he left instructions for his body to be boiled down so that all the fat could be extracted to make a candle. This candle, together with a passionate letter, was to be presented to the object of his unrequited affections. He stipulated that the letter and candle were to be delivered to the obdurate lady at night, so that she could read his final missive by the light of his "corpse candle".

"Only one man ever understood me. And he didn't understand me."

George Wilhelm Hegel (1770—1831), German philosopher.

"So little done.
So much to do!"

Alexander Graham Bell (1847—1922),
inventor of the telephone, who
was dictating a memo at the
time of his death.

Queen Elizabeth I (1533—1603), though she had lived a long and
eventful life, was not ready to die. She declared:

"All my possessions
for a moment of time."

13

Queen Caroline, neglected wife of George IV, drew up her will
just a few days before her death in 1821. At the same time she
sent for the undertaker to measure her for her coffin and
prepare the following inscription:

CAROLINE OF BRUNSWICK
Born 17th May, 1768,
Died 7th August, 1821.
Aged 54.
The outraged Queen of England.

The plate was removed by the authorities and replaced
with a more conventional memorial.

Selfless to the End

William Wycherley, author of The Country Wife and other plays,
lived from 1640 to 1715. At seventy-five, he married a young
woman, but died only eleven days after his wedding.
His last words to his wife were:

"Promise me you will never again marry an old man."

A young Kentucky woman directed in her will that tobacco should be planted on her grave, so that her bereaved lovers could smoke the leaves which her remains had nourished.

Lord Holland said:

"If Mr Selwyn calls, let him in; if I am alive I shall be very glad to see him, and if I am dead he will be very glad to see me."

Mr Selwyn was noted for his interest in viewing corpses and attending executions.

Daniel Webster (1782—1852), American statesman, said:

"Wife, children, doctor, I trust on this occasion I have said nothing unworthy of Daniel Webster."

John Huntingdon of Sawston, Cambridgeshire, left a will dated August 4th, 1554, in which he bequeathed his land and possessions to his heirs, on the condition that every year from then onwards, they sowed two acres of land with white peas, for the relief of the poor of the village.

The Ionian philosopher Anaxagoras (500—428 BC) was banished from Athens to Lampsacus. When he was on his deathbed, the citizens of his adopted home asked how they could pay tribute to his memory. His reply was:

"Give the boys a holiday."

His request was honoured and for many years the anniversary of his death was a holiday for all the schoolboys in Lampsacus.

Socrates (470?—399 BC), Athenian philospher said:

"Crito, I owe a cock to Aesculapius."

This could have been a way of asking his friend Crito to pay the doctor for his services: a cock was the usual offering made to Aesculapius, the god of medicine and healing.

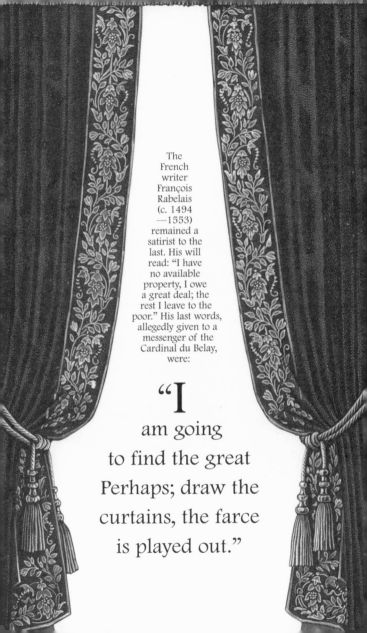

The French writer François Rabelais (c. 1494 —1553) remained a satirist to the last. His will read: "I have no available property, I owe a great deal; the rest I leave to the poor." His last words, allegedly given to a messenger of the Cardinal du Belay, were:

"I am going to find the great Perhaps; draw the curtains, the farce is played out."

Frederick the Great, Emperor of Prussia (1744—86) was passionately fond of his pet greyhounds. As he lay dying, he noticed one of his dogs shivering from the cold beside his bed and uttered these last words:

"Throw a quilt over it."

The American playwright Tennessee Williams (1911—1983) left a will which forbade any interference with his poems or his plays, which included Cat on a Hot Tin Roof, A Streetcar Named Desire, and The Night of the Iguana. He also left provision for "the comforts and pleasures" of his mentally-ill sister Rose, requesting that she might be allowed to enjoy shopping trips to New York City.

Even on his dying bed, King Charles II (1630—85) showed concern for his beloved mistress, Nell Gwynne. He said:

"Don't let poor Nelly starve."

King Henry VII (1457—1509) wanted his funeral to make a moral
statement. He asked his executors to have respect for:

"the laud and praising of God,
the health of our soul, and somewhat to
our dignity royal, but avoiding damnable
pomp and outrageous superfluities."

In his last will and testament,
Lodovico Cortusio,
who died on July 17th, 1418,
forbade any of his friends or relatives
to mourn openly at his funeral.
Anyone found weeping would be disinherited,
but the person who laughed most heartily
would be his principal heir
and universal legatee.
His funeral in the Church of Santa Sofia
in Padua was more like a wedding
than a wake.

Last-Minute Philosophers

We lean our heads on the pillow, and go out of the world in the same state of stupid amazement that we came into it!

William Hazlitt (1778—1830), English writer.

The dying words of the French philosopher Denis Diderot (1713—84) were:

"The first step towards philosophy is incredulity."

"The answer?
What is the answer?"
Pause. "In that case,
what is the question?"

This is one of the several published versions of the last words of the American writer Gertrude Stein (1874—1946).

"I don't know. I don't know."

Peter Abelard (1079—1152),
French philosopher and scholar,
and lover of Heloise.

There are conflicting accounts of the
last words spoken by the American poet
Emily Dickinson (1830—86).
One version is:

"I must go in, the fog is rising."

Another, supposedly in reference to a
drink of water she was offered, is:

"Oh, is that all it is?"

"Life is a woman that one loves, to whom we allow any condition in the world, so long as she does not leave us."

Giacomo Girolamo Casanova
(1725—1798), Italian adventurer
and writer. After working all over
Europe in a variety of jobs, he died
a librarian in Dux, Bohemia.

Sweet Revenge

John Hylett Stow, who died in 1781, left five guineas in his will for the purchase of a picture of a viper biting the benevolent hand of the person who had saved it from perishing in the snow. This picture was to be given to his lawyer, who he thought had shown "ingratitude and insolence" in return for his own "friendship and almost parental regard". The will prompted the lawyer to take the unusual step of commencing libel proceedings.

22

General Hawley drew up his own will because he hated all lawyers. He was not too fond of priests, either. His will instructed his executors to bury his "carcase" wherever they saw fit and to "let the puppy have it" should the parish priest ask for a burial fee.

A rich old bachelor, exasperated by the pressure exerted on him by his family to find a bride, developed such a hatred of women that he gave the following instruction in his will:

"I beg that my executors will see that I am buried where there is no woman interred, either to the right or to the left of me. Should this not be practicable in the ordinary course of things, I direct that they purchase three graves, and bury me in the middle one of the three, leaving the others unoccupied."

An Englishman who had always been strongly prejudiced against the Irish inherited a large plot of land in Tipperary, on the condition that he lived there. He grudgingly agreed to this disposition, but on his death in 1791, his will revealed how he wished to exact his revenge for this outrage. He bequeathed an annual sum of ten pounds, which was to be spent on whisky to be shared between up to twenty Irishmen. These men were to be taken to his graveside, each armed with a stick and a knife. His will concluded:

"**K**nowing what I know of the Irish character, my conviction is, that with these materials given, they will not fail to destroy each other, and when in the course of time the race comes to be exterminated, this neighbourhood at least may, perhaps, be colonized by civilized and respectable Englishmen."

Some Irish Curses

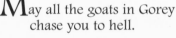

May your obituary
be written in weasel's piss.

May the lamb of God stir his
hoof through the roof of heaven
and kick you in the arse down to hell.

May the only tears at your graveside
be the onion-pullers'.

May all the goats in Gorey
chase you to hell.

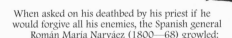

When asked on his deathbed by his priest if he
would forgive all his enemies, the Spanish general
Román María Narváez (1800—68) growled:

"I do not have to forgive my enemies.
I have had them all shot."

In the early 1900s, an American
doctor was incensed that his relatives,
who had ignored him during his lifetime,
had become extremely attentive when
they knew he was dying. Dr Wagner
decided to seek a gruesome revenge.
His will revealed that he had bequeathed
his left arm and hand to his brother,
Napoleon Bonaparte Wagner, and his
right arm and hand to his other brother,
George Washington Wagner. Other
relatives were to receive his nose, ears
and legs. Dr Wagner had thoughtfully
left a sum of a thousand dollars to pay
for the dismembering of his body.

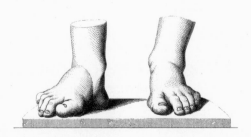

The American actress Joan Crawford (1908—77) disinherited two of her four adopted children in her will. However, one daughter, Christina Crawford Koontz, was able to retrieve her fortune and obtain revenge at one stroke by writing a best-selling book about the horrors of being brought up by her "Mommie Dearest".

John Hart, who died in 1765, left his brother a gun and a bullet

"In the hope that he will put the same through his head when the money is spent".

"My eldest son John having spoken disrepectfully of his little sister, whom I keep by me in Spirits of Wine, and in many other instances behaved himself undutifully towards me, I do disinherit, and wholly cut off from any Part of this my Personal Estate, by giving him a single Cockle-Shell."

Nicholas Gimcrack, Esq., early 1900s.

Wild & Whimsical

A Russian living in Odessa in the early 1900s left four million roubles to his four nieces, on the condition that they first work for a year as washerwomen, chambermaids or farm girls. The nieces carried out his wishes, but during their year of service they received over 860 proposals of marriage between them.

Valentine Tapley, owner of the longest beard in the world, died on April 2nd, 1910 at the age of eighty. The fame of his twelve-and-a half-foot beard was such that Mr Tapley feared that grave-robbers might break into his tomb to steal his whiskers. He therefore made provision in his will for an extra-strong tomb to prevent any post-mortem interference with his facial hair.

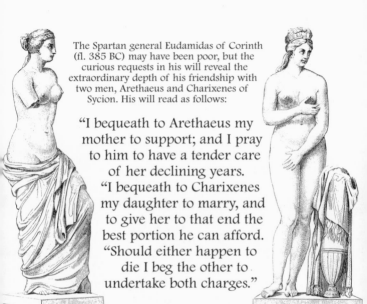

The Spartan general Eudamidas of Corinth (fl. 385 BC) may have been poor, but the curious requests in his will reveal the extraordinary depth of his friendship with two men, Arethaeus and Charixenes of Sycion. His will read as follows:

"I bequeath to Arethaeus my mother to support; and I pray to him to have a tender care of her declining years.
"I bequeath to Charixenes my daughter to marry, and to give her to that end the best portion he can afford.
"Should either happen to die I beg the other to undertake both charges."

Henry Budd, who died in 1862, left a will in which his sons, Edward and William, would be disinherited if they grew moustaches. A few years later, in 1869, Mr Fleming, an upholsterer of Pimlico, London, left ten pounds to each of his clean-shaven employees but only five pounds to those sporting moustaches.

I Nicholas Gimcrack, being in sound Health of Mind, but in great Weakness of Body, do by this my Last Will and Testament bequeath my worldly Goods and Chattels in Manner follows:
"Imprimis, To my dear Wife,
One Box of Butterflies,
One Drawer of Shells,
A Female Skeleton,
A dried Cockatrice.

"Item, To my Daughter Elizabeth,
My Receipt for preserving dead Caterpillars,
As also my preparations of Winter May-Dew,
and Embrio Pickle.

"Item, To my little Daughter Fanny,
Three Crocodiles' Eggs.
And upon the Birth of her first Child, if she marries with her Mother's Consent, The Nest of a Humming-Bird.

"Item, To my eldest Brother, as an Acknowledgement for the Lands he has vested in my Son Charles, I bequeath My last Year's Collection of Grasshoppers.

"Item, To his Daughter, Susanna, being his only Child, I bequeath my English Weeds pasted on Royal Paper, With my large Folio of Indian Cabbage ..."

Nicholas Gimcrack, Esq. This will appeared in Tatler in the early 1900s.

J uan Potomachi, who died in 1955,
   left £25,000 to a local theatre
on condition that they used his skull
     when performing Hamlet.

E. J. Halley of Memphis, Tennessee had used a huge sum
bequeathed to him by his foster mother to drink himself into an
early grave. When he died in 1910, he left money in his will to
sheriffs, favourite baseball players and orphanages, and also to
those who had apparently performed great services for him
during his last delirious days:

"To the nurse who kindly removed
a pink monkey from the foot of my bed,
$5000.

"To the cook at the hospital
who removed snakes from my broth,
$5000.

Needless to say, the will was contested by his relatives.

Professional
to the End

"Qualis artifex pereo!"
"What an artist dies in me!"

The Roman Emperor Nero Claudius Caesar (37—68)
died by his own hand, saying these words.

The French revolutionary leader Jacques Danton (1759—94),
who ordered thousands of guillotinings during the French
Revolution, was finally sentenced to a taste of his own medicine.
He told the executioner:

"Be sure to show the mob my head.
It will be a long time
before they see its like."

The escape artist and magician Harry
Houdini (1874—1926) left instructions
in his will for his executors to have his body
embalmed and placed in a vault identical to
his mother's. He also directed that a bronze
bust of himself should be placed on the
tomb, as this would facilitate his return
from the dead.

A nobleman of the
house of Du Châtelet
in France, who died
around 1280, requested
that one of the columns
in the church of
Neufchâteau should
be hollowed out
to receive his body,

"in order
that the
vulgar
may not
walk about
upon me."

Siward, the warrior Earl of Northumberland (?—1055) said:

"Lift me up that I may die standing,
not lying down like a cow."

"Get my swan costume ready!"

The Russian ballerina Anna Pavlova (1885—1931). She had made the dying swan dance from Swan Lake her signature piece.

Alex Wilson (1714—86),
Scottish-American ornithologist, requested:

"Bury me where the birds will sing over my grave."

The Russian pianist Vladimir Horowitz (1904—89) left $300,000 to the Juilliard School of Music, on the condition that there would never be a competition named after him.

"We are all going to Heaven, and Van Dyke is of the company."

The hope expressed by the English painter
Thomas Gainsborough (1727—88).

"I have offended God and mankind because my work did not achieve the quality it should have."

Leonardo da Vinci (1452—1520),
Italian painter and visionary.

The Roman Emperor Augustus said to his friends:

"Do you think I have played my part pretty well through the farce of life?"

The last words of Lady Mary Wortley Montagu (1689—1762), English poet and letter writer, were:

"It has all been very interesting."

Thomas Jefferson (1743—1826), third President of the United States, died on July 4th, 1826, exactly fifty years after the signing of the Declaration of Independence. He fell unconscious after asking:

"Is it the 4th?"

The last words of Andrew Bradford (1686—1742), publisher of the American Weekly Mercury, were:

"O Lord, forgive the errata!"

The French poet and critic Nicolas Boileau Despréaux (1636—1711) observed:

"It is of great consolation to a poet on the point of death that he has never written a line injurious to good morals."

In his will, the great Roman poet Virgil (70—19 BC) asked for the manuscripts of his epic poem, The Aeneid, to be burnt, as he felt that they contained many imperfections. His executors protested; so instead he bequeathed the manuscripts to them, on the condition that if he should die before he had time to revise and complete them, they should be published without amendments or additions from any other editor.

The American author Herman Melville (1819—91) spoke exactly the same last words as his character Billy Budd:

"God bless Captain Vere!"

A Yorkshire rector had been unhappy about his daughter's scandalous way of dressing. When he died in 1804, his will revealed that she would be disinherited if she did not dress with greater propriety than she had done during his lifetime. His greatest objection was to her habit of going about with bare forearms. This was to cease, or the inheritance would pass to her nephew. The rector wrote:

"Should anyone take exception to this my wish as being too severe, I answer that license in dress in a woman is a mark of a depraved mind."

Excessive Exits

"Alas, I am dying beyond my means."

Oscar Wilde (1854—1900),
Irish poet, wit and dramatist.

"I've had eighteen straight whiskies. I think that is the record."

Dylan Thomas (1914—53),
Welsh poet, who died of
what his doctors described
as a severe alcoholic
insult to his liver.

The Irish bard and composer Torlogh O'Carolan (1670—1738)
called for a glass of whisky, saying:

"It would be hard if two such friends
should part without at least one
sweet kiss."

"Too many cigars
this evening, I guess."

E. W. Scripps (1854—1926), American publisher.

Mr Davis of Clapham, London,
left the sum of five shillings

"to Mary Davis,
daughter of Peter
Delaport, which is
sufficient to enable
her to get drunk
for the last time
at my expense."

MENALIAE   ET   AGATHIAE
PARENTIBVS   SANCTISSIMIS
EPAPHRAS
POSTREMVM PRAESTITIT OFFICIVM
BIXIT ANN. XXXVI. M. I. D. IIX.   B. ANN. VL. M. IX. D. I.

Husbands & Wives

S FECIT SIBI ET LICINIAE ISAVRICAE CONIVGI
ATVRNINO ET LICINIAE BRASILANAE FIL.
ER. LIB.   POSTERISQVE.

Henry, Earl of Stafford, married the daughter of the Duc of Grammont at the end of the 17th century. She made his life a misery, as his will records:

"To the worst of women, Claude Charlotte de Grammont, unfortunately my wife, guilty as she is of all crimes, I leave five-and-forty brass halfpence, which will buy a pullet for her supper."

A British sailor requested his executors to pay his wife one shilling, with which to buy hazelnuts, as she had always preferred cracking nuts to mending his stockings.

In 1772, a Surrey Gentleman left the following will:

"Whereas it was my misfortune to be made very uneasy by ———, my wife, for many years from our marriage, by her turbulent behaviour, for she was not content to despise my admonitions, but she contrived every method to make me unhappy; she was so perverse in her nature that she would not be reclaimed, but seemed only to be born to be a plague to me; the strength of Samson, the knowledge of Homer, the prudence of Augustus, the cunning of Pyrrhus, the patience of Job, the subtlety of Hannibal and the watchfulness of Hermogenes could not have been sufficient to subdue her; for no skill or force in the world could make her good; and as we have lived separate and apart from each other for eight years, and, she having perverted her son to leave and totally abandon me, therefore, I give her a shilling."

44

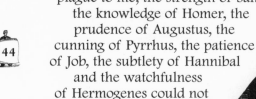

A Glasgow doctor, who died at the turn of the last century, had been deserted by his wife, and left his estate to his sisters. In his will, however, he asked his sister Elizabeth to provide his erring spouse with

"a gift of ten shillings sterling, to buy her a pocket handkerchief to weep after my decease."

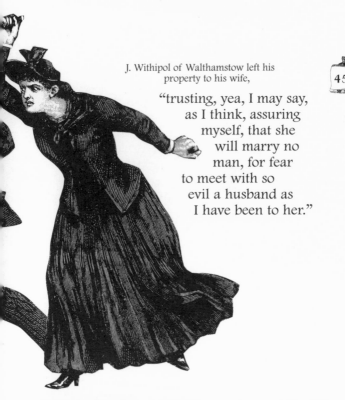

J. Withipol of Walthamstow left his property to his wife,

"trusting, yea, I may say, as I think, assuring myself, that she will marry no man, for fear to meet with so evil a husband as I have been to her."

Goods & Chattels

If a man dies without leaving a will, then all his property goes to the nearest villain. But if a man dies and leaves a will, then all his property goes to whoever can get possession of that will.

Jerome K. Jerome (1859—1927), English writer, on the laws of the stage.

It is a trial of skill between the legacy-hunter and the legacy-maker, which shall fool the other. The cringing toad-eater, the officious tale-bearer, is perhaps well paid for years of obsequious attendance with a bare mention and a mourning ring.

William Hazlitt (1778—1830), English writer.

The 1975 will of ex-mayor Edward Horley instructed his executors to cut a lemon in half and send one piece to the income tax inspectorate and the other to the tax collector with a message

"Now squeeze this".

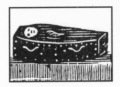

The will of Sieur Benôit, opened in Paris on October 8th, 1877, spared his executors the expense of a coffin:

"**I** expressly and formally desire that my remains may be enclosed for burial in my large leather trunk, instead of putting my survivors to the expense of a coffin. I am attached to that trunk, which has gone round the world with me three times."

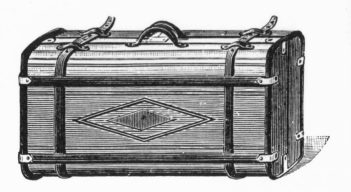

William Hickington, who died in 1770, left this will, which was
deemed legal by the Deanery Court in York:

This is my last will,
I insist on it still;
To sneer on and welcome,
And e'en laugh your fill.
I, William Hickington,
Poet of Pocklington,
Do give and bequeath,
As free as I breathe,
To thee, Mary Jarum,
The Queen of my Harum,
My cash and my cattle,
With every chattel,
To have and to hold,
Come heat or come cold,
Sans hindrance or strife,
Though thou art not
my wife ...

48

"You can keep the things of bronze
and stone and give me one man
to remember me just once a year."

Damon Runyan (1884—1946), American writer.

The relatives of a rich Irishman named
Dennis Tolam, who died in Cork in 1769,
were most displeased when his will was
read out, for in spite of his wealth, he
appeared to be bequeathing worthless
objects to his family. He left his sister
four old stockings, his nephew, two odd
socks and a green nightcap, and his
housekeeper, a broken water-jug.
However, when his disgruntled
housekeeper kicked the jug in
disgust, it broke to reveal a
stash of coins. The other relatives
hastily examined their bequests
and were relieved to find
similar piles of coins.

Bestial Conclusions

Henry David Thoreau (1817—62), American writer and naturalist, spoke words purportedly sounding like:

"Moose. Indian."

50

Jonathan Jackson of Columbus, Ohio, who died around 1880, left provision for the construction of a luxurious cats' home. He left detailed plans which included dormitories, a refectory, an infirmary, areas for conversation, roofs for climbing, rat-holes for sport, and an auditorium where inmates were to be assembled daily to listen to an accordion player.

Puss

Madame Dupuis, the famous 17th-century harpist,
who died in 1677, made ample provision for her beloved
cats in an otherwise vituperative and vindictive will.
She directed that her sister and her niece were to attend to
her cats. Her sister was to look after them, and the niece
to visit them three times a week. Among other provisions,
the feeding arrangements were to be as follows:

"They are to be served daily, in a
clean and proper manner,
with two meals of meat-soup, the same
as we eat ourselves, but it is to be given
them separately in two soup-plates.
The bread is not to be cut up into the
soup, but must be broken into squares
about the size of a nut, otherwise they
will refuse to eat it. A ration of meat,
finely minced, is to be added to it;
the whole is then to be mildly seasoned,
put into a clean pan, covered close,
and carefully simmered before it
is dished up ..."

a Hog

Saint Jerome speaks of a pig leaving a will, and this document
was first published by one Alexander Brassicanus, who died
in 1539. A further edition, based on a revised manuscript,
was published by G. Fabricius. According to his account,
the pig was condemned to a bloody slaughter by the cook,
for having smashed some small kitchen pots. When the pig
realized that his apologies and appeals for mercy had
fallen on deaf ears, he asked for an hour's grace to
write his will. The will is as follows:

52

"I, M. Grunnius Corcotta Porcellus,
have made my testament,
which, as I can't write myself,
I have dictated.
"I will and bequeath to my Papa,
Verrinus Lardinus,
thirty bushels of acorns.
"I will and bequeath to my Mamma,
Veturina Scrofa,
forty bushels of Laconian corn.
"I will and bequeath to my sister,
Quirona,
at whose nuptuals I may not be present,
thirty bushels of barley.

"Of my mortal remains,
I will and bequeath
my bristles to the cobblers,
my teeth to the squabblers,
my ears to the deaf,
my tongue to the lawyers
and chatterboxes,
my entrails to tripemen,
my hams to gluttons,
my stomach to little boys,
my tail to little girls,
my muscles to effeminate parties,
my heels to runners and hunters,
my claws to thieves;
and to a certain cook,
whom I won't mention by name,
I bequeath my cord and stick
which I brought with me
from my oak grove in the sty,
in hopes that he may take the cord
and hang himself with it."

The pig further directed that a monument be erected in his honour
and that his body should be embalmed with good condiments,
such as almonds, pepper and honey.

Pig

Pepper Box & Spoon

Spaniel

Phoebe Deliah Nye of Saint Louis, Missouri,
asked for her faithful dog, Lily, to be put to sleep
with chloroform after her death:

"It being my desire to spare her from ending her days without that care which she would receive if I were living."

Phoebe Nye also provided for drinking fountains
for both man and beast to be built in
various parts of the city.

A lady left seventy pounds a year for the
maintenance of her three goldfish, which
she identified as follows in her will:

"One is bigger than the other two, and these latter are to be easily recognized, as one is fat and the other lean."

She also made provision for flowers to be
placed upon the graves of the goldfish.

Bravehearts in a Brutal World

"This side is roasted enough, turn up,
O tyrant great;
Eat and see whether raw or roasted
I make better meat."

The 3rd-century Christian martyr, Saint Lawrence, to his
tormentors, as he was being roasted alive on a gridiron.

The English navigator and courtier
Sir Walter Raleigh (1552?—1618),
about to be beheaded, called for the axe
and felt its edge. He said:

**"It is a sharp medicine, but this is
that which cures all sorrows."**

Anne Boleyn (1507—36), the second
wife of Henry VIII, was accused of
adultery and beheaded. Just before
kneeling at the block, she circled
her neck with her hands, and said:

**"It is small,
very small
indeed."**

When King Louis XVI of France
(1754—93) was led to the
guillotine, he said to the crowd:

**"May my blood
cement your
happiness."**

Françoís Ravaillac (1578—1610), the assassin of the French King Henry IV, was found guilty of divine and human high treason. He was sentenced to have his skin torn with hot pincers and the wounds filled with molten lead and boiling oil. His right hand, holding the regicidal knife, was to be burned in a sulphur fire. Then he was to be torn to pieces, while still alive, by four horses, and to have his limbs reduced to ashes which would then be scattered to the winds. Ravaillac's request for a conditional absolution was granted, on the condition of eternal damnation if he turned out to have acted with accomplices, instead of alone, as he claimed. Ravaillac replied:

"I receive absolution upon this condition."

MARBURH IN HERMIONE.

Arria, wife of Caecina Paetus, committed suicide in 42 BC.
When the emperor commanded her husband to kill himself,
he hesitated. The brave Arria seized his dagger and plunged
it into her own breast. Then she withdrew it,
and handed it to him, saying:

"It doesn't hurt, Paetus."

"Smite my womb! Level your rage against the womb which gave birth to such a monster!"

The Roman Empress Agrippina (?15—59) to the
sword-wielding soldiers sent by her son Nero to murder her.

"I am just going outside
and may be some time."

The English explorer Lawrence E. G. Oates (1880—1912) to his
companions on Scott's ill-fated polar expedition. He walked into
certain death in the blizzard raging outside their tent.

The American poet Hart Crane (1899—1932)
dived from a passenger ship to drown himself, saying:

"Good-bye, everybody!"

"Don't cry. I need all my courage to die at twenty."

These were the words of the French mathematician
Evariste Galois (1811—32), mortally wounded in a duel.

Final Fears

William Sydney Porter (1862—1910),
American short-story writer, said:

"Turn up the lights.
I don't want to go home in the dark."

John Greenleaf Whittier (1807—92), American poet,
implored the nurse pulling the shades in his room:

"No! No!"

Many people have been frightened of waking up in their coffins, having been wrongly diagnosed as dead. It appears that the 14th-century Dukes of Lancaster were particularly afraid of being buried alive. Henry, who died in 1360, instructed in his will that his body should not be buried until three weeks after his death. John of Lancaster, usually known as John of Gaunt, specified that he should not be buried for forty days and that his corpse should not be embalmed.

The English novelist Wilkie Collins (1824—89) carried a letter requesting a second opinion should anyone declare him deceased. Harriet Martineau left ten pounds for her doctor, asking him to ensure that she was really dead before she was buried: by cutting her head off.

Edmund Yates, the novelist, left twenty guineas to whichever surgeon would slit his jugular before burial.

Jeremy Bentham, the English writer and jurist, who died in 1832, wanted his preserved corpse to be placed in a chair at the table of his colleagues when they met to discuss great matters

of philosophy. This wish was carried out to the letter, and the embalmed body of Bentham was dressed in his favourite hat. His face was covered by a wax mask. When not in use, the body was housed in a special mahogany case with a glass front, where it reposed in a large armchair. John Fuller, the MP, who died in1834, was afraid of being eaten by his loved ones. The worms, he thought, would eat him, and then ducks would eat the worms. His family would dine on the ducks ... So he was buried in a pyramid-shaped mausoleum, and, like Bentham, he was to spend eternity sitting up in an armchair, in his case with a glass of claret.

When the wick of his bedside
lamp flared up, the dying
French philosopher François
Marie Arouet de Voltaire
(1694—1778) asked:

"The flames already?"

Colonel Charteris said:

"I would gladly give £30,000 to have it proved to my satisfaction, that there is no such place as hell."

"**A**bove ground, I shall be food for the kites; below I shall be food for mole-crickets and ants. Why rob one to feed the other?"

The 4th-century Chinese philosopher, Chuang-Tzu, when asked how he would like to be buried.

The English poet John Keats (1795—1821), dying young of consumption, said:

"I feel the flowers growing over me."

The French writer George Sand (Amantine Aurore Dudevant) (1804—76) wanted her tomb to be left to nature, not covered with stone or bricks. She instructed:

"Laissez la verdure."
(Leave the greenery.)